To Alan Humm

SCORPIO

A guide to living your best astrological life

STELLA ANDROMEDA

ILLUSTRATED BY EVI O. STUDIO

Hardie Grant

BOOKS

Introduction 7

I.

Get to Know Scorpio

II.

The Scorpio Deep Dive

III.
Give Me More

Introduction

Inscribed on the forecourt of the ancient Greek temple of
Apollo at Delphi are the words 'know thyself'. This is one of
the 147 Delphic maxims, or rules to live by, attributed to Apollo
himself, and was later extended by the philosopher Socrates to
the sentence, 'The unexamined life is not worth living.'

People seek a variety of ways of knowing themselves, of
coming to terms with life and trying to find ways to understand
the challenges of human existence, often through therapy
or belief systems like organised religion. These are ways in
which we strive to understand the relationships we have with
ourselves and others better, seeking out particular tools that
enable us to do so.

As far as systems of understanding human nature and
experience go, astrology has much to offer through its symbolic
use of the constellations of the heavens, the depictions of the
zodiac signs, the planets and their energetic effects. Many
people find accessing this information and harnessing its
potential a useful way of thinking about how to manage
their lives more effectively.

What is astrology?

In simple terms, astrology is the study and interpretation of how the planets can influence us, and the world in which we live, through an understanding of their positions at a specific place in time. The practice of astrology relies on a combination of factual knowledge of the characteristics of these positions and their psychological interpretation.

Astrology is less of a belief system and more of a tool for living, from which ancient and established wisdom can be drawn. Any of us can learn to use astrology, not so much for divination or telling the future, but as a guidebook that provides greater insight and a more thoughtful way of approaching life. Timing is very much at the heart of astrology, and knowledge of planetary configurations and their relationship to each other at specific moments in time can assist in helping us with the timing of some of our life choices and decisions.

Knowing when major life shifts can occur – because of particular planetary configurations such as a Saturn return (see page 103) or Mercury retrograde (see page 104) – or what it means to have Venus in your seventh house (see pages 85 and 98), while recognising the specific characteristics of your sign, are all tools that you can use to your advantage. Knowledge is power, and astrology can be a very powerful supplement to approaching life's ups and downs and any relationships we form along the way.

The 12 signs of the zodiac

Each sign of the zodiac has a range of recognisable characteristics, shared by people born under that sign. This is your Sun sign, which you probably already know – and the usual starting point from which we each begin to explore our own astrological paths. Sun sign characteristics can be strongly exhibited in an individual's make-up; however, this is only part of the picture.

Usually, how we appear to others is tempered by the influence of other factors – and these are worth bearing in mind. Your ascendant sign is equally important, as is the positioning of your Moon. You can also look to your opposite sign to see what your Sun sign may need a little more of, to balance its characteristics.

After getting to know your Sun sign in the first part of this book, you might want to dive into the Give Me More section (see pages 74–105) to start to explore all the particulars of your birth chart. These will give you far greater insight into the myriad astrological influences that may play out in your life.

Sun signs

It takes 365 (and a quarter, to be precise) days for the Earth to orbit the Sun and in so doing, the Sun appears to us to spend a month travelling through each sign of the zodiac. Your Sun sign is therefore an indication of the sign that the Sun was travelling through at the time of your birth. Knowing what Sun signs you and your family, friends and lovers are provides you with just the beginning of the insights into character and personality that astrology can help you discover.

On the cusp

For those for whom a birthday falls close to the end of one Sun sign and the beginning of another, it's worth knowing what time you were born. There's no such thing, astrologically, as being 'on the cusp' – because the signs begin at a specific time on a specific date, although this can vary a little year on year. If you are not sure, you'll need to know your birth date, birth time and birth place to work out accurately to which Sun sign you belong. Once you have these, you can consult an astrologer or run your details through an online astrology site program (see page 108) to give you the most accurate birth chart possible.

Taurus

The bull

✦

21 APRIL–20 MAY

Grounded, sensual and appreciative of bodily pleasures, Taurus is a fixed earth sign endowed by its ruling planet Venus with grace and a love of beauty, despite its depiction as a bull. Generally characterised by an easy and uncomplicated, if occasionally stubborn, approach to life, Taurus' opposite sign is watery Scorpio.

Aries

The ram

✦

21 MARCH–20 APRIL

Astrologically the first sign of the zodiac, Aries appears alongside the vernal (or spring) equinox. A cardinal fire sign, depicted by the ram, it is the sign of beginnings and ruled by planet Mars, which represents a dynamic ability to meet challenges energetically and creatively. Its opposite sign is airy Libra.

Gemini

The twins

✴

21 MAY–20 JUNE

A mutable air sign symbolised by the twins, Gemini tends to see both sides of an argument, its speedy intellect influenced by its ruling planet Mercury. Tending to fight shy of commitment, this sign also epitomises a certain youthfulness of attitude. Its opposite sign is fiery Sagittarius.

Cancer

The crab

✴

21 JUNE–21 JULY

Depicted by the crab and the tenacity of its claws, Cancer is a cardinal water sign, emotional and intuitive, its sensitivity protected by its shell. Ruled by the maternal Moon, the shell also represents the security of home, to which Cancer is committed. Its opposite sign is earthy Capricorn.

Leo

The lion

★

22 JULY–21 AUGUST

A fixed fire sign, ruled by the Sun, Leo loves to shine and is an idealist at heart, positive and generous to a fault. Depicted by the lion, Leo can roar with pride and be confident and uncompromising, with a great faith and trust in humanity. Its opposite sign is airy Aquarius.

Virgo

The virgin

★

22 AUGUST–21 SEPTEMBER

Traditionally represented as a maiden or virgin, this mutable earth sign is observant, detail oriented and tends towards self-sufficiency. Ruled by Mercury, Virgo benefits from a sharp intellect that can be self-critical, while often being very health conscious. Its opposite sign is watery Pisces.

Scorpio
The scorpion
★

22 OCTOBER–21 NOVEMBER

Given to intense feelings, as
befits a fixed water sign, Scorpio
is depicted by the scorpion – linking
it to the rebirth that follows death –
and is ruled by both Pluto and Mars.
With a strong spirituality and deep
emotions, Scorpio needs security to
transform its strength. Its opposite
sign is earthy Taurus.

Libra
The scales
★

22 SEPTEMBER–21 OCTOBER

A cardinal air sign, ruled by Venus,
Libra is all about beauty, balance
(as depicted by the scales) and
harmony in its rather romanticised,
ideal world. With a strong aesthetic
sense, Libra can be both arty and
crafty, but also likes fairness and
can be very diplomatic. Its
opposite sign is fiery Aries.

Sagittarius

The archer

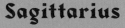

✷

22 NOVEMBER–21 DECEMBER

Depicted by the archer, Sagittarius is a mutable fire sign that's all about travel and adventure, in body or mind, and is very direct in approach. Ruled by the benevolent Jupiter, Sagittarius is optimistic with lots of ideas; liking a free rein, but with a tendency to generalise. Its opposite sign is airy Gemini.

Capricorn

The goat

✷

22 DECEMBER–20 JANUARY

Ruled by Saturn, Capricorn is a cardinal earth sign associated with hard work and depicted by the sure-footed and sometimes playful goat. Trustworthy and unafraid of commitment, Capricorn is often very self-sufficient and has the discipline for the freelance working life. Its opposite sign is the watery Cancer.

Aquarius

The water carrier

★

21 JANUARY–19 FEBRUARY

Confusingly, given its depiction
by the water carrier, Aquarius
is a fixed air sign ruled by the
unpredictable Uranus, sweeping
away old ideas with innovative
thinking. Tolerant, open-minded
and all about humanity, its vision
is social with a conscience. Its
opposite sign is fiery Leo.

Pisces

The fish

★

20 FEBRUARY–20 MARCH

Acutely responsive to its
surroundings, Pisces is a mutable
water sign depicted by two fish,
swimming in opposite directions,
sometimes confusing fantasy with
reality. Ruled by Neptune, its
world is fluid, imaginative and
empathetic, often picking up on
the moods of others. Its opposite
sign is earthy Virgo.

Get to

I.

Know

Scorpio

The sign the Sun was travelling in at the time you were born is the ultimate starting point in exploring your character and personality through the zodiac.

Fixed water sign,
depicted by the scorpion.

Ruled by Pluto, the ancient god
of the underworld, there is a
powerful connection between
Scorpio and the cycle of life.

OPPOSITE SIGN

Taurus

STATEMENT OF SELF

'I desire.'

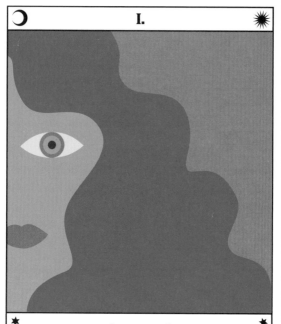

I.

Lucky colour

Deep reds, crimsons and burgundy colours, resonating with a passionate energy that is often buried but needs expression in Scorpio. Wear these colours when you need a psychological boost and additional courage. If you don't want to be ostentatious with such a bold colour, choose red accessories – shoes, gloves, socks, hat or even underwear.

Lucky day

Tuesday. Named after Mars, the god of war, we see this more obviously in the French word for Tuesday, *Mardi*. Although ruled by Pluto, Scorpio is also associated with the strong planet Mars, which is why Tuesday is their lucky day.

Lucky gem

Topaz comes in many colours. It resonates strongly
with a spiritual energy and is thought to be healing and
regenerative. It also echoes those traits in Scorpio that are
aligned to a powerful and sometimes secretive inner life.

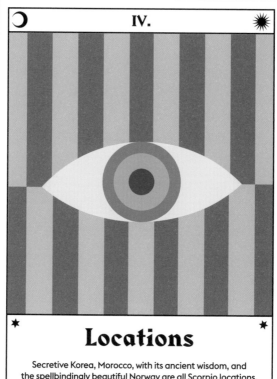

Locations

Secretive Korea, Morocco, with its ancient wisdom, and
the spellbindingly beautiful Norway are all Scorpio locations.
Others include Finland, the Transvaal of South Africa and
Bavaria. Astrologically beneficial cities for Scorpio include
New Orleans, Liverpool, Dubrovnik and Washington DC.

Holidays

Scorpio relishes exploring the underworld to
recharge their batteries, whether this is the physical world
of underwater diving in the Seychelles or a flotation tank
in an upmarket Scandinavian spa resort. Exploring the
archaeological mysteries of ancient Egypt or a silent
Buddhist meditation or yoga retreat in Goa might also
appeal to Scorpio's mystical side.

Flowers

The chrysanthemum is Scorpio's flower. It blooms in autumn and is often associated with regeneration and the powerful rebirth of spring that follows autumn and winter, while its deeply-coloured or brightly-golden blooms have a powerful longevity.

Trees

Blackthorn, with its spiky thorns, is a plant with a sting in it, reflecting the scorpion. It is actually a member of the rose family, with beautiful creamy-white flowers that give way to small, dark blue, plum-like sloes, with an astringent taste used to make sloe gin.

VIII.

Pets

The intense loyalty of a dog appeals to Scorpio, especially one that is possessive about its owner and appears to read their mind, knowing when to encourage activity and when to rest peacefully alongside them.

IX.

Parties

A secret destination, mysterious décor, a dark and
sexy basement club, all appeal to Scorpio's idea of what
makes for a great party. Masks to hide identities and play
out fantasies may also be a theme. Certainly there's often
an unexpected punch or sting in the tail of Scorpio's choice
of cocktails, embodied in an assertive mezcal Negroni
with its smoky agave flavour.

Scorpio characteristics

The saying that 'still waters run deep' often provides a first clue about Scorpio, because what you see isn't necessarily what you get with this water sign. There is usually so much hidden in the waves beneath their apparently calm surface – no wonder they appear secretive. Despite this, and even when emotions *are* being expressed, there's also a deep inner streak of calm, connected to their emotional depth from which they get their stability. Scorpio is considered one of the most powerful (and occasionally difficult) Sun signs: a real poker player, there's just so much going on inside that's not always obvious to those around them. They need solitude to process all this internal activity and this occasional need to withdraw can give them a reputation for being moody. What's going on inside their heads is often as real to them as anything else but it's sometimes difficult to share, and they respond to this with further intensity. All that imagination has to find an outlet, though, and the smart Scorpio will learn to harness this to inspire their personal creativity.

You can't go far with Scorpio without being reminded (probably by them!) that this sign rules the genitals, linking the power of sexual attraction to the life force and regeneration that stems from procreation. The life force in Scorpio operates not only on a physical but also on a mental level, and for them sex is often about communication and healing as much as about superficial pleasure. Scorpio's reputation for magnetism (sexual or otherwise) stems from their keenly intuitive nature and ability to gauge other people's moods, being so familiar as they are with the intensity of their own.

Another facet of Scorpio that's not always easily understood is their idealism. They actually believe in the best and can be very positive about life – this also stems from a sense of regeneration, that anything can be improved upon or made anew, even if it seems impossible to everyone else. And in this idealism lies an intensity of belief seldom matched by others. This can make Scorpio one of the kindest, most loyal and even gentlest of signs, which is sometimes unexpected; and as much as they thrive in sexual relationships, their friendships are equally important and often as intense.

SOFTENING THE WATER

The key characteristics of any
Sun sign can be balanced out
(or sometimes reinforced) by the
characteristics of other signs in the
same birth chart, particularly those
of the ascendant and the Moon. So
if someone doesn't appear to be
typical of their Sun sign, that's why.
However, those nascent Scorpio
aspects will always be there as
a key influence, informing an
individual's approach to life.

Physical Scorpio

There's an intense physical energy about Scorpio that's often immediately apparent from the way they move: decisively and definitely. Their bodies suggest strength, even if their build is slight, and they tend towards leanness rather than bulk. But, unlike their fellow watery-souled crustacean Cancer, who takes a sideways route, Scorpio tends to take a straightforward fast-paced route, direct from A to B. Even when their bodies are still, and Scorpio can keep intensely still, they're absorbing the world around them with a keen-eyed focus on what's going on. Not much escapes Scorpio's notice.

Health

Inevitably, given that Scorpio rules the genitals and reproductive organs, this can be an area of weakness for them. But the life force, their energy in general, can also be affected in other ways and Scorpio is a sign that tends to over-extend themselves, going all-out, over-doing it, and then collapsing with exhaustion before regenerating and replenishing their energy reserves. In time, they do eventually learn not to burn the candle at both ends! This tendency towards overdoing it can extend to Scorpio's mental health, where exhaustion can also take its toll. Emotional burnout can arise from the intensity with which Scorpio approaches life, so learning to respect that desire for occasional solitude to recharge their batteries is important.

Exercise

Watery exercise appeals and Scorpio often finds that swimming is not only meditative but also restorative to both body and soul. It's important to Scorpio for any exercise to balance body and mind, making regular yoga and t'ai chi attractive to them, too. Building muscle isn't greatly of interest to Scorpio, but building stamina is, in an effort to protect and support their energy.

How Scorpio communicates

Scorpio doesn't really do small talk, talking about the weather bores them and they'd rather get straight to the nitty gritty of 'How are you?' and expect you to do the same. This can make for some intense conversations and they can also be provocative in an effort to spark an interesting exchange. They may keep their own cards close to their chest, though, getting the other person to spill the beans without really realising it. Unlike some, however, Scorpio really is keen to know what you think and will listen, often really thinking about what you've said and coming up with a relevant (and sometimes left-field) response. As confidantes go, Scorpio's take on a situation can sometimes surprise, but they seldom give a glib answer. This can make for some fascinating conversations, often late into the night, and digging deep for answers to big questions.

Scorpio careers

Whatever Scorpio does, they are usually attracted to work that involves the mind, body and soul, because for them it all tends to be linked. While power fascinates them, Scorpio is often more of a 'back room' type – the political advisor or analyst rather than the prime minister – and they don't mind this just as long as they aren't bored. Given their inclination towards the mind, psychology and its off-shoots often attract Scorpio, sometimes drawing them into psychoanalytical careers to connect with the deeply buried unconscious. That same psychological approach can be applied elsewhere and to sex therapy, too.

Digging deep and finding out about anything tends to interest Scorpio, though, so research work of some sort – scientific or detective – has a strong appeal, as does journalism, which is all about asking questions and getting to the root of a story. Because they often have a pragmatic approach to life and death, medicine can also interest Scorpio, maybe in work as a fertility specialist or obstetrician, or in other sorts of healing occupations through alternative therapies.

How Scorpio chimes

From lovers to friends, when it comes to other signs, how does Scorpio get along? Knowledge of other signs and how they interact can be helpful when negotiating relationships, revealed through an understanding of Sun sign characteristics that might chime or chafe. Understanding these through an astrological framework can be really helpful as it can depersonalise potential frictions, taking the sting out of what appears to be in opposition.

Scorpio is all about feelings, and often very intense ones at that, which isn't always easy for them or their partners and lovers. They need to feel needed, and respond well when there is a lot of give and take. But it's just not possible to live 100 percent of the time at full emotional throttle, and as Scorpio matures in their relationships, they can learn to recognise this and trust those who function at a lower level of intensity.

The Scorpio woman

Emotional and demanding, it's easy to forget how loyal and affectionate the Scorpio woman can be. But she is also possessive, unlikely to forgive and forget. This isn't a woman looking for a brief affair, that's not how she operates, so she probably won't waste her time on a fling. Her magnetism is often in her eyes, which are penetrating in their look.

NOTABLE SCORPIO WOMEN

Remember Julia Roberts in *Pretty Woman*? Scorpio personified. Other mesmeric Scorpios include US politician Hillary Clinton, who famously 'stood by her man' Bill, and poet Sylvia Plath, whose intensity resulted in her enduring work (and marriage to fellow poet Ted Hughes). Kendall Jenner, Emma Stone and Katy Perry are all characteristically captivating Scorpio women, too.

The Scorpio man

Sensual, but often insecure, the Scorpio man is not the easiest to live with. He tends to dominate a room even when silent; and is naturally curious, giving the object of his affection full attention – and expecting it in return. His vulnerability lies in his tender heart; it's all or nothing when it comes to love. And he hates ambiguity, so don't mess with him unless you're serious.

Actor Adam Driver has the brooding look of Scorpio, as does Leonardo di Caprio and Ryan Gosling. Entrepreneur Bill Gates and painter Pablo Picasso both show that obsessive commitment to their passion, while Prince Charles' enduring love for Camilla is a Scorpio trait, too.

Who love

s whom?

Scorpio & Aries

Sexual sparks fly between these two, and there's much to get this attraction going, but overall Scorpio's more emotional, secretive side tends to exasperate open-hearted and free-spirited Aries, who can seem a little superficial to the deeper-minded water sign.

Scorpio & Taurus

There's a shared trait of stubbornness and jealousy here that could cause problems, which would be a shame because Scorpio relishes Taurus' earthy desire and sexual stamina, and Taurus enjoys the deeper emotional connection.

Scorpio & Gemini

There's an element of flightiness to Gemini that can undermine Scorpio's need for total commitment, and this challenge to their emotional security might outweigh the initial attraction Scorpio has to a more social butterfly.

Scorpio & Cancer

Scorpio's need for affection and devotion is well matched by Cancer's need for security, and while the crab can be rather passive, it responds well to Scorpio's possessiveness and passionate ardour, making this a well-matched combination.

Scorpio & Leo

The physical attraction is very strong, but Leo's extravagance and need for romantic gestures is at odds with Scorpio's need for a deeper erotic connection, which creates a potential clash that could be difficult to overcome between these two driven types.

Scorpio & Virgo

Deep feelings and a natural inclination toward commitment in both these signs create a bond on which a good relationship can be built, as long as Virgo doesn't try to restrict the more intellectual or sensual aspects of Scorpio's personality.

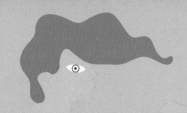

Scorpio & Scorpio

Unless they recognise that it is their similarities that create difficulties from the word go, this pairing will eventually sting their relationship to death with a mismatch of moods, secrets and possessiveness, in spite of their sexual compatibility.

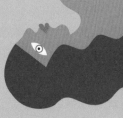

Scorpio & Libra

This can be a tricky pairing because while Libra is interested by Scorpio's intellectual and sexual intensity, Scorpio's need for commitment isn't easily met by Libra, who finds Scorpio's inclination to be jealous and too demanding.

Scorpio & Sagittarius

At first, Sagittarius' freewheeling, fun-loving attitude is deeply attractive to Scorpio, but it will rankle in time if Scorpio's need for security isn't met because of Sagittarius' constant pursuit of travel and new adventures in body and mind.

Scorpio & Aquarius

Scorpio's deep, emotional demands conflict with Aquarius' open-hearted approach to love (and sex), and Scorpio finds this intellectual airiness undermining, tending to make them feel too insecure to tolerate anything more than a brief affair.

Scorpio & Pisces

There's a nice balance here between Scorpio's strong, silent aspect and Pisces' rather indecisive take on life, while their sexual attraction is a highly imaginative, romantic one and their tendency to feel emotions deeply makes them both feel secure.

Scorpio & Capricorn

Both signs are equally serious about being on the same emotional team, with an almost equal need for security, while Scorpio's passionate intensity balances Capricorn's more brooding approach to sex, making this a compatible pairing.

Scorpio love-o-meter

Least compatible

Scorpio   Aquarius   Libra   Gemini   Aries   Leo

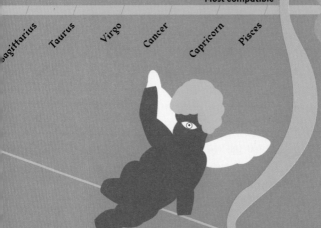

Sagittarius   Taurus   Virgo   Cancer   Capricorn   Pisces

Most compatible

The Scorpio

II.

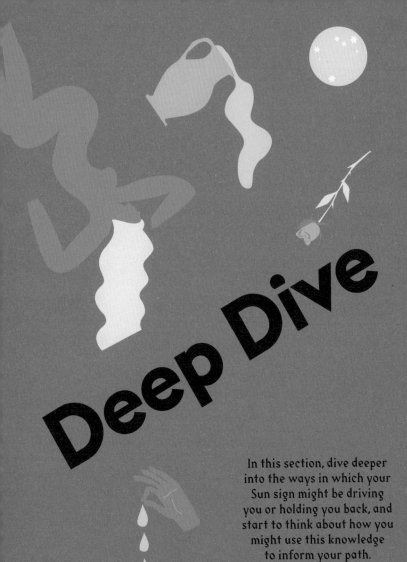

Deep Dive

In this section, dive deeper into the ways in which your Sun sign might be driving you or holding you back, and start to think about how you might use this knowledge to inform your path.

The
Scorpio
home

There's something of a need for Scorpio to burrow deep into domesticity from time to time, and their home may reflect this with dark, womb-like interiors of crimson, terracotta or deep pink colours; with velvet furnishings and a sense of intense seclusion in which they can revitalise. The bedroom, particularly, may represent something of a haven, a healing zone even, full of items of desire, opulent and luxurious. The bed large with beautiful linen, Persian rugs on the floor, interesting pictures on the wall. Not for Scorpio a minimalist Scandinavian ascetism. And this often extends to the bathroom, itself a possible place of ritual and somewhere this water sign can connect with their inner life, candlelit and with bath oils.

Possessive about their privacy, a Scorpio invitation is not casually given as their home very much represents their secret side. There may even be a basement den, study or workshop. House parties are of little interest to Scorpio and any socialising at home is likely to be with a select few, one-to-one even, where deep conversations can be enjoyed.

TOP TIPS FOR
SCORPIO SELF-CARE

* Emotional downtime is
  important to recharge and
  regenerate, so factor it in.

* Sensual hands-on therapies
  can also facilitate reconnecting
  body and mind.

* Set boundaries. All that
  absorbing other people's
  energy can sap Scorpio's.

Self-care

With everything that's going on inside their head, Scorpio has to remember to gently reconnect body and mind occasionally. All that intensity of thought means they can sometimes neglect their bodies, and this can become self-destructive, promoting the sort of stress that can lead to anxiety and depression. With an inclination towards intensity, however, there's also a tendency to become a tad obsessive with any self-care regime, which can sometimes get a bit heavy-handed: self-care is supposed to promote well-being and relieve stress, Scorpio, not increase it. Balancing different activities can help: a gentle hike one day, a spin class the next. Less inclined towards socialising through exercise, team sports can be a challenge for Scorpio, but a one-to-one tennis match could appeal.

Regular meals and wholefoods, fresh fruit and vegetables, rather than snacking, are helpful to Scorpio, keeping both the mind *and* blood sugar levels on an even keel, and balancing out all that nervous energy. Hands-on therapies should appeal, especially the more sensuous of massages, as they work to promote the sort of deep relaxation that Scorpio can sometime find tricky. Sleep can sometimes elude Scorpio, as their heads whir excessively at 3 a.m., and this too has to be managed.

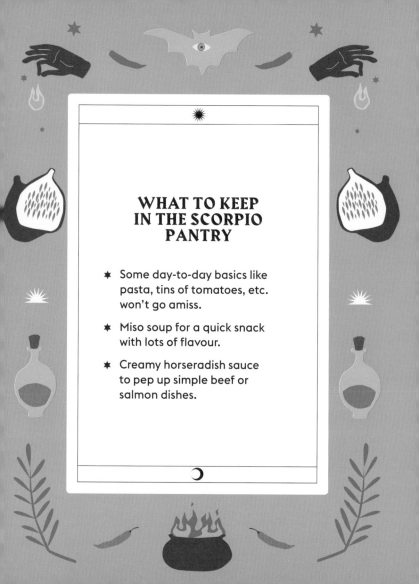

WHAT TO KEEP IN THE SCORPIO PANTRY

★ Some day-to-day basics like pasta, tins of tomatoes, etc. won't go amiss.

★ Miso soup for a quick snack with lots of flavour.

★ Creamy horseradish sauce to pep up simple beef or salmon dishes.

Food
and
cooking

For Scorpio, day-to-day food is more about sustenance and a way of rejuvenating their energy, rather than sheer gourmet pleasure. They can't be bothered to sweat in the kitchen merely for the sake of culinary enjoyment and that can make them rather mundane cooks with a poorly stocked fridge, except when it comes to trying to seduce someone. Then they are likely to use their transformation skills to turn a chicken casserole into a delicious Provençal coq au vin. Then, food, cooking and eating is all about its sensual qualities and intense flavours, but Scorpio isn't, generally, the classic sign of a cook. In fact, even when they're on the seduction trail, they might keep it simple, sourcing the finest figs, the ripest Camembert, the best Serrano ham, the most succulent steak, relying on high-quality ingredients to enhance their reputation in the kitchen rather than any personal mastery or technique.

TOP TIPS FOR
SCORPIO'S MONEY

* Being thrifty shouldn't be at the expense of having fun: have a fund for that, too.

* Secret off-shore accounts are one thing but keep savings legal.

* Back your hunches, as that Scorpio intuition could pay off.

How Scorpio handles money

Scorpio is pretty adept when it comes to money, even hiding a stash in a secret account to protect against lean times. Money is important to Scorpio because it represents self-value and respect rather than what it can buy, plus it can provide the wherewithal to transform situations – and Scorpio is all about transformation. The Scorpio penchant for sensing undercurrents, and considering the influences that may affect markets, means there are few risky ventures or investments.

Day to day, Scorpio's competitive edge makes them canny at work, with an eye on a good salary and bonus schemes. They are also often lucky with inheritances, legacies and windfalls that might result from someone else's death. Saving is a natural inclination, although Scorpio doesn't penny pinch and is happy to splash out occasionally for something they have planned for, whether it's the holiday of a lifetime or a Rolex watch, although they don't particularly value luxuries for luxury's sake.

How Scorpio handles the boss

Playing their cards close to the chest comes so easily to Scorpio that they are often the office confidante, including the boss'. People tell them things, about which Scorpio remains so discreet, they're never considered a gossip. That's quite a powerful asset to have, as long as it's not exploited, but smart Scorpios can be relied upon to keep their own counsel and the boss will recognise this. The only thing that can feel like a bit of a threat is that possible sting in the tail: will Scorpio go after the boss' job? Maybe, but only if it's strategically beneficial to them, as many Scorpios prefer to be the power *behind* the throne, not actually sitting on it and taking the rap.

Because of their loyalty, Scorpio can be someone on whom a boss can rely, just as long as their interest is held. In getting what they want from a job, Scorpio needs to handle their boss' expectations but also let them know what they need in order to deliver. And because one of Scorpio's skills is for transformation, using that to turn hard work into a material asset that can improve a business' bottom line can ensure the sort of recognition that can lead to promotion.

TOP TIPS TO
HANDLE THE BOSS

* Never gossip, so the boss knows Scorpio is to be trusted.

* Be the power behind the throne, but don't exploit it.

* Remember that the sting in Scorpio's tail is a last resort, not a first strategy.

TOP TIPS FOR
AN EASIER LIFE

★ Don't assume everyone can
  second guess your mood:
  communicate!

★ Channel energy into your
  gentle, loyal and sunny side
  for happy times.

★ Remember that not everything
  has to be perfect: don't sweat
  the small stuff.

What is Scorpio like to live with?

Scorpio often overlooks the quirks of housemates or partners because they are curious about and ready to consider the reasons behind other people's behaviours. This can make them open-minded and easy to live with, unless this trait is exploited. Abuse it and that sting could be lethal!

It's also true that while Scorpio doesn't suffer fools gladly, they often keep their own counsel and will just disappear from a situation they don't like. This can give Scorpio the reputation for being moody, but if they don't want to continue a discussion or participate socially, they won't. This isn't sulking, just a need to replenish their inner energy, which can get sapped by too many demands. Time out and time alone is often the way Scorpio will recuperate, and this need shouldn't be taken personally.

This complex mix of needing lots of intense one-to-one communication, coupled with a need for privacy, can be perplexing to those living with Scorpio. Scorpio needs to remember that how they're feeling isn't always obvious to others, who may misjudge the situation as a consequence.

How to handle a break-up

The downside of the need for a deep connection to another person, and Scorpio's tendency toward possessiveness, can make a break-up very difficult indeed. Trust is always an issue for Scorpio. It may not look like it, but a lot of work has gone on before they trust someone, so if this is betrayed it's always hard. Scorpio is also a fixed sign, so adjusting to *any* change is tricky, and something has to be really dead before they will let go. There is often a series of attempts to bring a relationship back to life before finally letting it go, and this can prolong the agony.

TOP TIPS FOR AN EASIER BREAK-UP

★ If the relationship is clearly over, let it go.

★ It is possible to transform a relationship into a friendship, but it takes time.

★ Bury yourself in distractions until you feel better. You will.

How Scorpio wants to be loved

Scorpio wants to be loved completely, passionately, emotionally and physically – that's all! If that sounds like a tall order, then it's because they are given to being the most intense sign of the zodiac, prepared to invest everything in a relationship that they hope will sustain them on every level. While the physical side of love features hugely in Scorpio's profile, on account of this sign being said to rule the genitals, it isn't limited to this. The emotional side is as important to Scorpio, sometimes even more so, and is always a feature of their commitment and one that they will expect in equal measure in return.

None of this is necessarily obvious, thanks to Scorpio's secretive side. Ruled by Pluto, the god of the underworld, Scorpio may struggle to convey how they want to be loved, and this may make them feel very vulnerable and sometimes unnecessarily defensive. The focus of their desire may have no idea how Scorpio feels, until they choose to strike. And, once they've declared themselves, Scorpio would like immediate reciprocation on which to base their trust. This can be tricky as it can take others, especially those who are more cautious about love, a while to catch up and feel as equally in love as Scorpio. For sanity's sake, Scorpio must remember this, otherwise they are likely to assume a rejection when none exists, just because their partner doesn't show immediate commitment.

Loving Scorpio can be intensely rewarding but their constant need for reassurance can be difficult to understand. Because everything has to be so deep and meaningful for Scorpio, it constantly raises questions for them. The answer to the question may always be the same, 'Yes, I love you,' but it won't stop the need to raise it. Trust takes a while to establish for Scorpio and it can sometimes feel to their partner as if their commitment is being constantly challenged. It may be. Fortunately, once Scorpio does feel loved and feels that their devotion, affection and loyalty are reciprocated, they can relax.

Scorpio uses physical love to convey what's sometimes hard to express verbally and often has the expectation that this be fully reciprocated. This is how they feel love is transformed, and loving them will involve sharing a regular, explorative and expressive sex life, using the body to make an almost psychic connection.

TOP TIPS FOR
LOVING SCORPIO

★ Show your love in deeds as well as words, as Scorpio seldom takes it for granted.

★ Be prepared to share every emotion; Scorpio won't expect anything less.

★ Don't deliberately provoke Scorpio's possessive side, it could backfire.

Scorpio's sex life

There's a real chamber of secrets to be explored with Scorpio, but it's also important to remember that sex isn't just about the physical side of love for them, or not very often. Usually there's a strong spiritual undertow to sex for Scorpio, and its transformative power to change or secure a relationship means that a one-night stand is of little interest. Sex for them usually has to be within the terms of a relationship towards which they (if not their partner) have already made a commitment.

Once in bed, however, there can be an intensity and passion seldom matched by other signs, but also a playful curiosity and willingness to listen and explore a partner's needs as much as their own, making them great in bed. However, this isn't the sign of straightforward foreplay, it's always a bit of a mysterious dance which may need to be played out long before getting to sex. In fact, because of their secretive side, Scorpio may appear to give more than they receive in bed, at least initially, but it's also their way of encouraging their partner's commitment. Long intense looks, lots of kissing and caressing, Scorpio likes to savour every sensual moment.

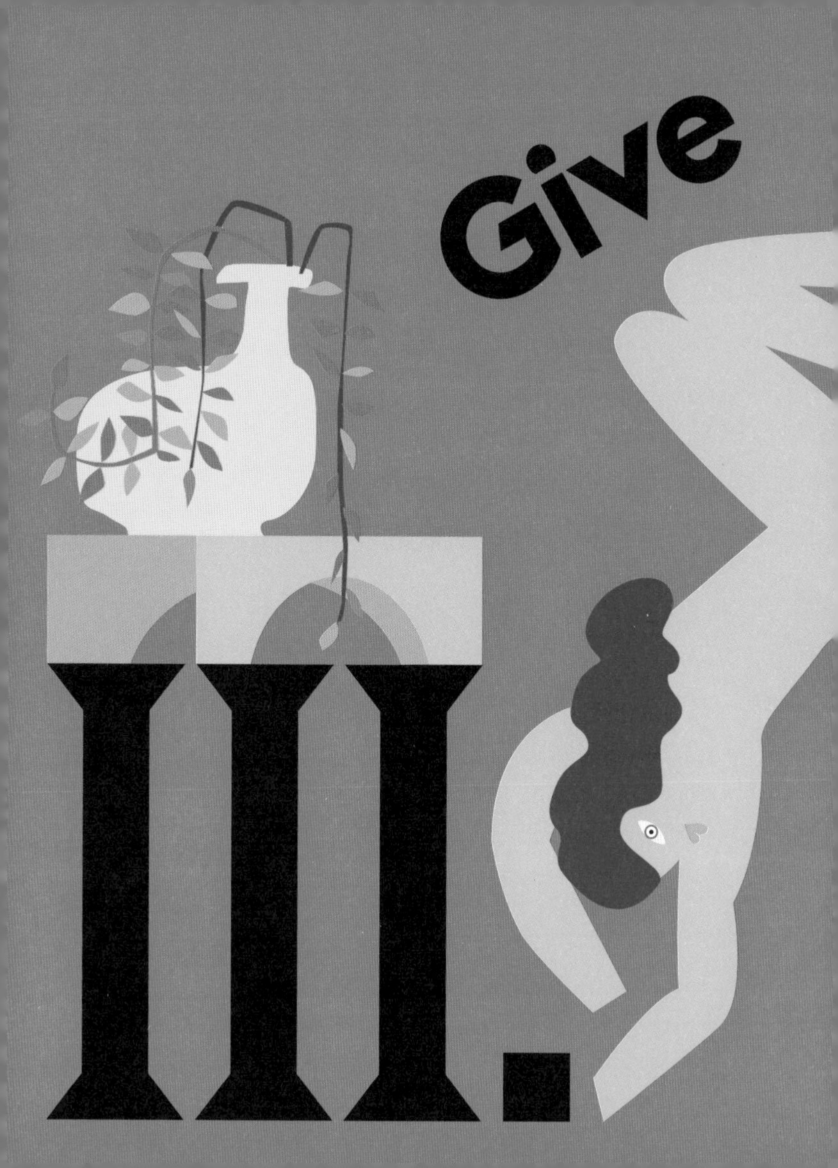
Give
III.

Me More

Your Sun sign never shows you the whole picture. In this section, learn how to read the nuances of your birth chart and discover a whole new level of astrological insight.

Your birth chart

Your birth chart is a snapshot of a particular moment, in a particular place, at the precise moment of your birth and is therefore completely individual to you. It's like a blueprint, a map, a statement of occurrence, spelling out possible traits and influences – but it isn't your destiny. It is just a symbolic tool to which you can refer, based on the position of the planets at the time of your birth. If you can't get to an astrologer, these days anyone can get their birth chart prepared in minutes online (see page 108 for a list of websites and apps that will do it for you). Even if you don't know your exact time of birth, just knowing the date and place of birth can create the beginnings of a useful template.

Remember, nothing is intrinsically good or bad in astrology and there is no explicit timing or forecasting: it's more a question of influences and how these might play out positively or negatively. And if we have some insight, and some tools with which to approach, see or interpret our circumstances and surroundings, this gives us something to work with.

When you are reading your birth chart, it's useful to first understand all the tools of astrology available to you; not only the astrological signs and what they represent, but also the 10 planets referred to in astrology and their individual characteristics, along with the 12 houses and what they mean. Individually, these tools of astrology are of passing interest, but when you start to see how they might sit in juxtaposition to each other, then the bigger picture becomes more accessible and we begin to gain insights that can be useful to us.

Broadly speaking, each of the planets suggests a different type of energy, the astrological signs propose the various ways in which that energy might be expressed, while the houses represent areas of experience in which this expression might operate.

Next to bring into the picture are the positions of the signs at four key points: the ascendant, or rising sign, and its opposite, the descendant; and the midheaven and its opposite, the IC, not to mention the different aspects created by congregations of signs and planets.

It is now possible to see how subtle the reading of a birth chart might be and how it is infinite in its variety, and highly specific to an individual. With this information, and a working understanding of the symbolic meaning and influences of the signs, planets and houses of your unique astrological profile, you can begin to use these tools to help with decision-making and other aspects of life.

Reading your chart

If you have your birth chart prepared, either by hand or via an online program, you will see a circle divided into 12 segments, with information clustered at various points indicating the position of each zodiac sign, in which segment it appears and at what degree. Irrespective of the features that are relevant to the individual, each chart follows the same pattern when it comes to interpretation.

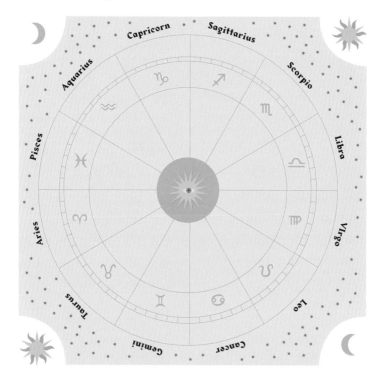

Given the time of birth, the place of birth and the position of the planets at that moment, the birth chart, sometimes called a natal horoscope, is drawn up.

If you consider the chart as a clock face, the first house (see pages 95–99 for the astrological houses) begins at the 9, and it is from this point that, travelling anti-clockwise the chart is read from the first house, through the 12 segments of the chart to the twelfth.

The beginning point, the 9, is also the point at which the Sun rises on your life, giving you your ascendant, or rising sign, and opposite to this, at the 3 of the clock face, is your descendant sign. The midheaven point of your chart, the MC, is at 12, and its opposite, the IC, at 6 (see pages 101–102).

Understanding the significance of the characteristics of the astrological signs and the planets, their particular energies, their placements and their aspects to each other can be helpful in understanding ourselves and our relationships with others. In day-to-day life, too, the changing configuration of planets and their effects are much more easily understood with a basic knowledge of astrology, as are the recurring patterns that can sometimes strengthen and sometimes delay opportunities and possibilities. Working with, rather than against, these trends can make life more manageable and, in the last resort, more successful.

The
Moon
effect

If your Sun sign represents your consciousness, your life force and your individual will, then the Moon represents that side of your personality that you tend to keep rather secret or hidden. This is the realm of instinct, intuition, creativity and the unconscious, which can take you places emotionally that are sometimes hard to understand. This is what brings great subtlety and nuance to a person, way beyond just their Sun sign. So you may have your Sun in Scorpio, and all that means, but this might be countered by a strongly practical and grounded Moon in Taurus; or you may have your Sun in open-hearted Leo, but a Moon in Aquarius with all its rebellious, emotional detachment.

Phases of the Moon

The Moon orbits the Earth, taking roughly 28 days to do so. How much of the Moon we see is determined by how much of the Sun's light it reflects, giving us the impression that it waxes, or grows, and wanes. When the Moon is new, to us, only a sliver of it is illuminated. As it waxes, it reflects more light and moves from a crescent, to a waxing crescent to a first quarter; then it moves to a waxing gibbous Moon, to a full Moon. Then the Moon begins to wane through a waning gibbous, to a last quarter, and then the cycle begins again. All of this occurs over four weeks. When we have two full Moons in any one calendar month, the second is called a blue Moon.

Each month the Moon also moves through an astrological sign, as we know from our personal birth charts. This, too, will yield information – a Moon in Scorpio can have a very different effect to one in Capricorn – and depending on our personal charts, this can have a shifting influence each month. For example, if the Moon in your birth chart is in Virgo, then when the actual Moon moves into Virgo, this will have an additional influence. Read the characteristics of the signs for further information (see pages 12–17).

The Moon's cycle has an energetic effect, which we can see quite easily on the ocean tides. Astrologically, because the Moon is both a fertility symbol and attuned to our deeper psychological side, we can use this to focus more profoundly and creatively on aspects of life that are important to us.

Eclipses

Generally speaking, an eclipse covers up and prevents light being shed on a situation. Astrologically speaking, this will depend on where the Sun or Moon is positioned in relation to other planets at the time of an eclipse. So if a solar eclipse is in Gemini, there will be a Geminian influence or an influence on Geminis.

Hiding, or shedding, light on an area of our lives is an invitation to pay attention to it. Eclipses are generally about beginnings or endings, which is why our ancestors saw them as portents, important signs to be taken notice of. As it is possible to know when an eclipse is forthcoming, these are charted astronomically; consequently, their astrological significance can be assessed and acted upon ahead of time.

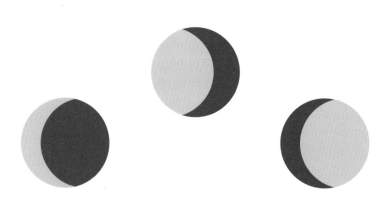

The 10 planets

For the purpose of astrology (but not for astronomy, because the Sun is really a star) we talk about 10 planets, and each astrological sign has a ruling planet, with Mercury, Venus and Mars each being assigned two. The characteristics of each planet describe those influences that can affect signs, all of which information feeds into the interpretation of a birth chart.

The Moon

This sign is an opposing principle to the Sun, forming a pair, and it represents the feminine, symbolising containment and receptivity, how we react most instinctively and with feeling.

Rules the sign of Cancer.

The Sun

The Sun represents the masculine, and is seen as the energy that sparks life, which suggests a paternal energy in our birth chart. It also symbolises our self or essential being, and our purpose.

Rules the sign of Leo.

Mercury

Mercury is the planet of communication and symbolises our urge to make sense of, understand and communicate our thoughts through words.

Rules the signs of Gemini and Virgo.

Venus

The planet of love is all about attraction, connection and pleasure and in a female chart it symbolises her style of femininity, while in a male chart it represents his ideal partner.

Rules the signs of Taurus and Libra.

Mars

This planet symbolises pure energy (Mars was, after all, the god of War) but it also tells you in which areas you're most likely to be assertive, aggressive or to take risks.

Rules the signs of Aries and Scorpio.

Saturn

Saturn is sometimes called the wise teacher or taskmaster of astrology, symbolising lessons learnt and limitations, showing us the value of determination, tenacity and resilience.

Rules the sign of Capricorn.

Jupiter

The planet Jupiter is the largest in our solar system and symbolises bounty and benevolence, all that is expansive and jovial. Like the sign it rules, it's also about moving away from the home on journeys and exploration.

Rules the sign of Sagittarius.

Uranus

This planet symbolises the unexpected, new ideas and innovation, and the urge to tear down the old and usher in the new. The downside can mark an inability to fit in and consequently the feeling of being an outsider.

Rules the sign of Aquarius.

Pluto

Aligned to Hades (*Pluto* in Latin), the god of the underworld or death, this planet exerts a powerful force that lies below the surface and which, in its most negative form, can represent obsessions and compulsive behaviour.

Rules the sign of Scorpio.

Neptune

Linked to the sea, this is about what lies beneath, underwater and too deep to be seen clearly. Sensitive, intuitive and artistic, it also symbolises the capacity to love unconditionally, to forgive and forget.

Rules the sign of Pisces.

The four elements

Further divisions of the 12 astrological signs into the four
elements of earth, fire, air and water yield other characteristics.
This comes from ancient Greek medicine, where the body was
considered to be made up of four bodily fluids or 'humours'.
These four humours – blood, yellow bile, black bile and phlegm
– corresponded to the four temperaments of sanguine, choleric,
melancholic and phlegmatic, to the four seasons of the year,
spring, summer, autumn, winter, and the four elements of air,
fire, earth and water.

Related to astrology, these symbolic qualities cast further
light on characteristics of the different signs. Carl Jung also
used them in his psychology, and we still refer to people
as earthy, fiery, airy or wet in their approach to life, while
sometimes describing people as 'being in their element'. In
astrology, those Sun signs that share the same element are said
to have an affinity, or an understanding, with each other.

Like all aspects of astrology, there is always a positive and a
negative, and a knowledge of any 'shadow side' can be helpful
in terms of self-knowledge and what we may need to enhance
or balance out, particularly in our dealings with others.

Air

GEMINI ✳ LIBRA ✳ AQUARIUS

The realm of ideas is where these air signs excel. Perceptive and visionary and able to see the big picture, there is a very reflective quality to air signs that helps to vent situations. Too much air, however, can dissipate intentions, so Gemini might be indecisive, Libra has a tendency to sit on the fence, while Aquarius can be very disengaged.

Fire

ARIES ✳ LEO ✳ SAGITTARIUS

There is a warmth and energy to these signs, a positive approach, spontaneity and enthusiasm that can be inspiring and very motivational to others. The downside is that Aries has a tendency to rush in headfirst, Leo can have a need for attention and Sagittarius can tend to talk it up but not deliver.

Earth

TAURUS ✳ VIRGO ✳ CAPRICORN

Characteristically, these signs enjoy sensual pleasure, relishing food and other physical satisfactions, and they like to feel grounded, preferring to base their ideas in facts. The downside is that Taureans can be stubborn, Virgos can be pernickety and Capricorns can veer towards a dogged conservatism.

Water

CANCER ✳ SCORPIO ✳ PISCES

Water signs are very responsive, like the tide ebbing and flowing, and can be very perceptive and intuitive, sometimes uncannily so because of their ability to feel. The downside is – watery enough – a tendency to feel swamped, and then Cancer can be both tenacious and self-protective, Pisces chameleon-like in their attention and Scorpio unpredictable and intense.

Cardinal, fixed and mutable signs

In addition to the 12 signs being divided into four elements, they can also be grouped into three different ways in which their energies may act or react, giving further depth to each sign's particular characteristics.

Cardinal

ARIES ✳ CANCER ✳ LIBRA ✳ CAPRICORN

These are action planets, with an energy that takes the initiative and gets things started. Aries has the vision, Cancer the feelings, Libra the contacts and Capricorn the strategy.

Fixed

TAURUS ✳ LEO ✳ SCORPIO ✳ AQUARIUS

Slower but more determined, these signs work to progress and maintain those initiatives that the cardinal signs have fired up. Taurus offers physical comfort, Leo loyalty, Scorpio emotional support and Aquarius sound advice. You can count on fixed signs, but they tend to resist change.

Mutable

GEMINI ✳ VIRGO ✳ SAGITTARIUS ✳ PISCES

Adaptable and responsive to new ideas, places and people, mutable signs have a unique ability to adjust to their surroundings. Gemini is mentally agile, Virgo is practical and versatile, Sagittarius visualises possibilities and Pisces is responsive to change.

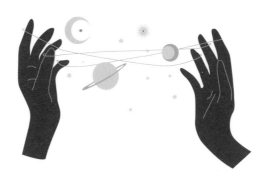

The 12 houses

The birth chart is divided into 12 houses, which represent separate areas and functions of your life. When you are told you have something in a specific house – for example, Libra (balance) in the fifth house (creativity and sex) – it creates a way of interpreting the influences that can arise and are particular to how you might approach an aspect of your life.

Each house relates to a Sun sign, and in this way each is represented by some of the characteristics of that sign, which is said to be its natural ruler.

Three of these houses are considered to be mystical, relating to our interior, psychic world: the fourth (home), eighth (death and regeneration) and twelfth (secrets).

1st House

THE SELF

RULED BY ARIES

This house symbolises the self: you, who you are and how you represent yourself, your likes, dislikes and approach to life. It also represents how you see yourself and what you want in life.

2nd House

POSSESSIONS

RULED BY TAURUS

The second house symbolises your possessions, what you own, including money; how you earn or acquire your income; and your material security and the physical things you take with you as you move through life.

3rd House

COMMUNICATION

RULED BY GEMINI

This house is about communication and mental attitude, primarily how you express yourself. It's also about how you function within your family, and how you travel to school or work, and includes how you think, speak, write and learn.

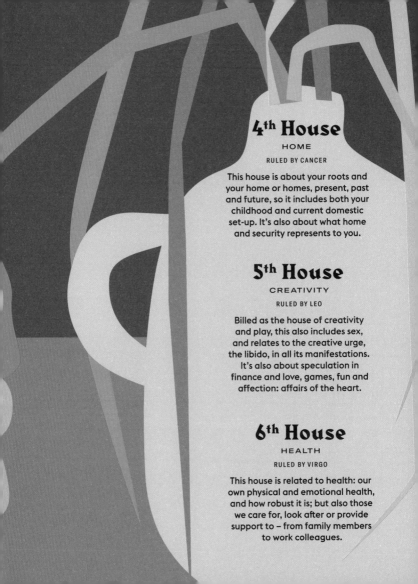

4ᵗʰ **House**

HOME

RULED BY CANCER

This house is about your roots and your home or homes, present, past and future, so it includes both your childhood and current domestic set-up. It's also about what home and security represents to you.

5ᵗʰ **House**

CREATIVITY

RULED BY LEO

Billed as the house of creativity and play, this also includes sex, and relates to the creative urge, the libido, in all its manifestations. It's also about speculation in finance and love, games, fun and affection: affairs of the heart.

6ᵗʰ **House**

HEALTH

RULED BY VIRGO

This house is related to health: our own physical and emotional health, and how robust it is; but also those we care for, look after or provide support to – from family members to work colleagues.

7th House

PARTNERSHIPS

RULED BY LIBRA

The opposite of the first house, this reflects shared goals and intimate partnerships, our choice of life partner and how successful our relationships might be. It also reflects partnerships and adversaries in our professional world.

8th House

REGENERATION

RULED BY SCORPIO

For death, read regeneration or spiritual transformation: this house also reflects legacies and what you inherit after death, in personality traits or materially. And because regeneration requires sex, it's also about sex and sexual emotions.

9th House

TRAVEL

RULED BY SAGITTARIUS

The house of long-distance travel and exploration, this is also about the broadening of the mind that travel can bring, and how that might express itself. It also reflects the sending out of ideas, which can come about from literary effort or publication.

11th House

FRIENDSHIPS

RULED BY AQUARIUS

The eleventh house is about friendship groups and acquaintances, vision and ideas, and is less about immediate gratification but more concerning longer-term dreams and how these might be realised through our ability to work harmoniously with others.

12th House

SECRETS

RULED BY PISCES

Considered the most spiritual house, it is also the house of the unconscious, of secrets and of what might lie hidden, the metaphorical skeleton in the closet. It also reflects the secret ways we might self-sabotage or imprison our own efforts by not exploring them.

10th House

ASPIRATIONS

RULED BY CAPRICORN

This represents our aspiration and status, how we'd like to be elevated in public standing (or not), our ambitions, image and what we'd like to attain in life, through our own efforts.

The ascendant

Otherwise known as your rising sign, this is the sign of the zodiac that appears at the horizon as dawn breaks on the day of your birth, depending on your location in the world and time of birth. This is why knowing your time of birth is a useful factor in astrology, because your 'rising sign' yields a lot of information about those aspects of your character that are more on show, how you present yourself and how you are seen by others. So, even if you are a Sun Scorpio, but have Cancer rising, you may be seen as someone who is maternal, with a noticeable commitment to the domestic life in one way or another. Knowing your own ascendant – or that of another person – will often help explain why there doesn't seem to be such a direct correlation between their personality and their Sun sign.

As long as you know your time of birth and where you were born, working out your ascendant using an online tool or app is very easy (see page 108). Just ask your mum or other family members, or check your birth certificate (in those countries that include a birth time). If the astrological chart were a clock face, the ascendant would be at the 9 o'clock position.

The descendant

The descendant gives an indication of a possible life partner, based on the idea that opposites attract. Once you know your ascendant, the descendant is easy to work out as it is always six signs away: for example, if your ascendant is Virgo, your descendant is Pisces. If the astrological chart were a clock face, the descendant would be at the 3 o'clock position.

The midheaven (MC)

Also included in the birth chart is the position of the midheaven or MC (from the Latin, *medium coeli,* meaning middle of the heavens), which indicates your attitude towards your work, career and professional standing. If the astrological chart were a clock face, the MC would be at the 12 o'clock position.

The IC

Finally, your IC (from the Latin, *imum coeli,* meaning the lowest part of the heavens) indicates your attitude towards your home and family, and is also related to the end of your life. Your IC will be directly opposite your MC: for example, if your MC is Aquarius, your IC is Leo. If the astrological chart were a clock face, the IC would be at the 6 o'clock position.

Saturn return

Saturn is one of the slower-moving planets, taking around 28 years to complete its orbit around the Sun and return to the place it occupied at the time of your birth. This return can last between two to three years and be very noticeable in the period coming up to our thirtieth and sixtieth birthdays, often considered to be significant 'milestone' birthdays.

Because the energy of Saturn is sometimes experienced as demanding, this isn't always an easy period of life. A wise teacher or a hard taskmaster, some consider the Saturn effect as 'cruel to be kind' in the way that many good teachers can be, keeping us on track like a rigorous personal trainer.

Everyone experiences their Saturn return relevant to their circumstances, but it is a good time to take stock, let go of the stuff in your life that no longer serves you and revise your expectations, while being unapologetic about what you would like to include more of in your life. So if you are experiencing or anticipating this life event, embrace and work with it because what you learn now – about yourself, mainly – is worth knowing, however turbulent it might be, and can pay dividends in how you manage the next 28 years!

Mercury retrograde

Even those with little interest in astrology often take notice when the planet Mercury is retrograde. Astrologically, retrogrades are periods when planets are stationary but, as we continue to move forwards, Mercury 'appears' to move backwards. There is a shadow period either side of a retrograde period, when it could be said to be slowing down or speeding up, which can also be a little turbulent. Generally speaking, the advice is not to make any important moves related to communication on a retrograde and, even if a decision is made, know that it's likely to change.

Given that Mercury is the planet of communication, you can immediately see why there are concerns about its retrograde status and its link to communication failures – of the old-fashioned sort when the post office loses a letter, or the more modern technological variety when your computer crashes

– causing problems. Mercury retrograde can also affect travel, with delays in flights or train times, traffic jams or collisions. Mercury also influences personal communications: listening, speaking, being heard (or not), and can cause confusion or arguments. It can also affect more formal agreements, like contracts between buyer and seller.

These retrograde periods occur three to four times a year, lasting for roughly three weeks, with a shadow period either side. The dates in which it happens also mean it occurs within a specific astrological sign. If, for example, it occurs between 25 October and 15 November, its effect would be linked to the characteristics of Scorpio. In addition, those Sun sign Scorpios, or those with Scorpio in significant placements in their chart, may also experience a greater effect.

Mercury retrograde dates are easy to find from an astrological table, or ephemeris, and online. These can be used in order to avoid planning events that might be affected around these times. How Mercury retrograde may affect you more personally requires knowledge of your birth chart and an understanding of its more specific combination of influences with the signs and planets in your chart.

If you are going to weather a Mercury retrograde more easily, be aware that glitches can occur so, to some extent, expect delays and double-check details. Stay positive if postponements occur and consider this period an opportunity to slow down, review or reconsider ideas in your business or your personal life. Use the time to correct mistakes or reshape plans, preparing for when any stuck energy can shift and you can move forward again more smoothly.

Further reading

Astrology Decoded (2013) by Sue Merlyn Farebrother; published by Rider

Astrology for Dummies (2007) by Rae Orion; published by Wiley Publishing

Chart Interpretation Handbook: Guidelines for Understanding the Essentials of the Birth Chart (1990) by Stephen Arroyo; published by CRCS Publications

Jung's Studies in Astrology (2018) by Liz Greene; published by RKP

The Only Astrology Book You'll Ever Need (2012) by Joanne Woolfolk; published by Taylor Trade

Websites

astro.com

astrologyzone.com

jessicaadams.com

shelleyvonstrunkel.com

Apps

Astrostyle

Co-Star

Susan Miller's Astrology Zone

The Daily Horoscope

The Pattern

Time Passages

Acknowledgements

Particular thanks are due to my trusty
team of Taureans. Firstly, to Kate Pollard,
Publishing Director at Hardie Grant, for her
passion for beautiful books and for commissioning
this series. And to Bex Fitzsimons for all her good
natured and conscientious editing. And finally to
Evi O. Studio, whose illustration and design talents
have produced small works of art. With such a
star-studded team, these books can only
shine and for that, my thanks.

About the author

Stella Andromeda has been studying
astrology for over 30 years, believing that
a knowledge of the constellations of the
skies and their potential for psychological
interpretation can be a useful tool. This
extension of her study into book form makes
modern insights about the ancient wisdom
of the stars easily accessible, sharing her
passion that reflection and self-knowledge
only empowers us in life. With her sun in
Taurus, Aquarius ascendant and Moon
in Cancer, she utilises earth, air and water
to inspire her own astrological journey.

Published in 2019 by Hardie Grant Books,
an imprint of Hardie Grant Publishing

Hardie Grant Books (London)
5th & 6th Floors
52–54 Southwark Street
London, SE1 1UN

Hardie Grant Books (Melbourne)
Building 1, 658 Church Street
Richmond, Victoria 3121

hardiegrantbooks.com

All rights reserved. No part of this publication may be reproduced,
stored in a retrieval system or transmitted in any form by any
means, electronic, mechanical, photocopying, recording or
otherwise, without the prior written permission of
the publishers and copyright holders.

The moral rights of the author have been asserted.

Copyright text © Stella Andromeda
Copyright illustrations © Evi O. Studio

British Library Cataloguing-in-Publication Data. A catalogue record
for this book is available from the British Library.

Scorpio
ISBN: 9781784882662

20 19 18 17 16 15 14 13
Publishing Director: Kate Pollard
Junior Editor: Bex Fitzsimons
Art Direction and Illustrations: Evi O. Studio
Editor: Wendy Hobson
Production Controller: Sinead Hering

Colour reproduction by p2d
Printed and bound in China by Leo Paper Products Ltd.